y wife Jean of 53 years, my beautiful and talented daughters Andrea and Amie, in-law) Archie Allen, and mother-in-law Albertina Dawkins, thank you for your vering support and love; my Aunt Bennie Lee and Uncle James "Tom" Seekers deceased) who were my second parents and will always hold a special place in eart; and my late mother Aver Lee, who in spite of the shame and ridicule she d giving birth to me, I owe an eternal debt of gratitude. ~ James Otis

o my parents James and Jean Morehead who gifted me the love for writing. ll that I am is because of you! ~ Love, Andrea

Publisher: Clover Lane Media, LLC

ummary: For over 70 years, James O. Morehead has endured taunting, teasing, d stares by people who often ask him, "What are you?" He explains how icking out from the rest is a special gift from God. He hopes anyone who feels ullied or ostracized will use his experience to find hope and inspiration to know hey were created by God for a special purpose - to let their light shine!

ISBN: 978-1-7353467-7-9 (Hardcover)
978-1-7353467-8-6 (Softcover)
978-1-7353467-9-3 (Ebook)

The
Brightest

by Andrea Morehead and James Mo

Illustrated by
Stephanie Hider

Forew
Marvin J
of the CW
"Black Lig

To m
son (
unw
(both
my h
face

S
a
s
b
t

There are so many shades of people around the world
It is part of God's wonderful tapestry He's twirled
To help teach us how we can all get along
Just like the different harmonies in a song

When people see me
They might take a double take
Because I am different and there are not a lot of people
Who look like how God decided to make

So, I want to let you know
About the wonderful things about me that glow
Remember, like you, I am part of His master plan
To bring people together to better understand
Why He creates us all in His image
In hopes that our differences will link us together
Through understanding and acceptance
Which is why I write this to you
I call my love letter

James Otis Morehead

If you're reading this book right now it's because you are gifted, you are strong, you are beauty, and you are truth. At any age you are youth. The wonder of God's love you truly are the proof. Being different is what makes us all special being born, then born again to be better. The foolish made wise, and the weak made mighty. The light of my soul, the light of the world. The Brightest Star.

I Corinthians 1:27 - "But God chose the foolish things of the world to shame the wise and the weak things of the world to shame the strong."

Marvin Jones III "Black Lightning"

One in 20,000 people in North America and Europe are known as an albino.

Here's a clever way to remember how to say it, and here goes.

A guy like me named **Al** said,
> "**By no** means should you be ashamed for a gene in your body did not produce the color of your race. And it's still a blessing that God made you by His saving grace."

I have lighter skin
that is bright white.
As a child I would be
teased and, of course,
you know that is not right.

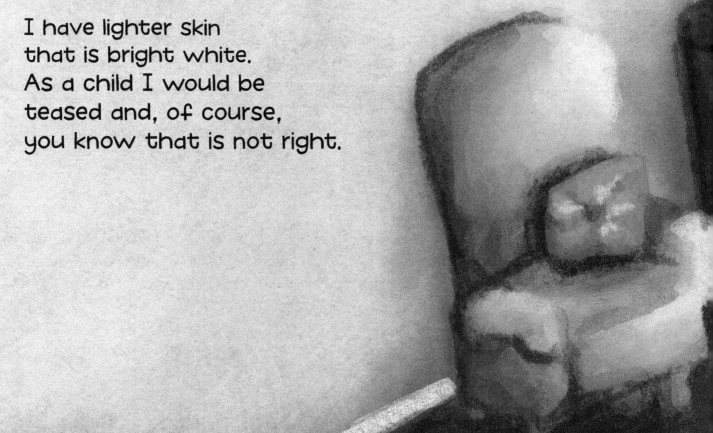

I was called all kinds of names, not James, but words that really hurt. The worst ones were "Red" because the sun would burn my skin all over my body including my chin.

Other names were "Ghost" and "Casper," "White Boy," "Snow Boy," and even "Snow Flake." It didn't matter what the kids used because all of them made my heart ache.

Almost every day on the playground I was all alone and bullied by kids screaming, "You need to get a tan." Every night I cried myself asleep hoping that God would help them understand that being different actually made me unique!

It is very important to speak positive words to yourself which is part of building up your self-esteem. God placed the right people in my life who became a special part of my team.

I had an Uncle named Tom who really believed in me.
And he always said, "James Otis, you can become
whatever you want to be."

My hair is golden like blonde
with highlights that look
kissed by the sun.
As I've gotten older
it's turned grey
which means
I have wisdom
so that is okay,
Because God has
proven that my
outside shell does
not tell the full story of
how my life was meant
to bring Him glory.

The color of my eyes are light
which makes them sensitive especially
when things are bright.
I have always worn eyeglasses
since I was a little boy,
and God has filled my life
with so much joy.

It hasn't been easy finding true friends
especially the kind who want to see you win.
So, it never dawned on me that
I would ever find my person
fearing there would be toward me an aversion.
But God had me at the right place at the right time
to meet a beautiful young lady to dine.

We met in theater class and acted in plays at Grambling State University...

where I found other friends who treated me with respect and dignity.

After a lot of time courting
I knew Jean stood for all things
right just and fair. I asked her
to marry me and she said, "Yes!"
She was God's answer to my prayer.

She's not just my wife but my
best friend placed in my life for a reason.
And for that I have loved her and always will
until the end of our season.

Then came our two children Andrea and Amie.

I taught them that although
I'm a different color
my race and culture are black.
They have a darker hue
and always have my back.

That's what family is all about.
No matter our differences we all can shout
about the goodness of God and
how He requires all of us to be kind.

So here's a little bit more
I need to get off my mind.

My Uncle Tom was right.
You can be anything you want to be.
No matter what anyone says,
as long as you believe you can achieve.

I had a dream of becoming a famous
actor on Broadway in New York,
the city that never sleeps.
That didn't happen.
But God's promises of purpose He keeps.
I still followed my passion and
became a college professor
of theater and speech.

"He was my favorite and most inspirational professor at Anderson University."

Mia Goins

"His class shaped me to this day and how I communicate publicly."

Brian Mack

"Genuine and always very kind toward his students."

Christian Ingram

Imagine the kid who didn't like
people looking at him has stood
in front of thousands of students,
and teaching them to never fear
and project their best and always
lean on God for the rest.
I often get calls or messages from the students
as far back as the 1980's thanking me for giving them
confidence to shine bright. I don't take the credit,
instead, I honor Him for being my guiding light.

I never thought that I would someday become a preacher.
Studying God's word, writing sermons,
and educating people is another form of a teacher.

My favorite scripture is Isaiah 40:31:
    "They who wait for the Lord shall renew their strength:
    They shall mount up with wings like eagles,
    They shall run and not be weary,
    They shall walk and not be faint."

The moral of my story is that God
has not given us the spirit of ain'ts.
Just fly like the eagle with courage and power,
and do not ever fall prey to being a coward.

To whom much is given much is required.
I choose joy and not to be mired
in negativity, but instead share positivity.

Like the young albino in my hometown of Anderson, Indiana.
He was sad and sometimes mad about his skin color
and not being able to be out in the sun.

I told him, "You might turn red and get blisters,
but you can always count on me as your soul Mister,
who prays for you and with you because I understand.
And like me you will make it through and become a
purposeful man, who's chosen to show the world
that with God you can."

There are other types of albinos that have skin without color, like snakes, tigers, giraffes and alligators, all beings great and small. But we want you to know that we stand proud and tall.

You may also see us as models and in movies, but we're not a fad and not a trend. Albinos are intentionally made and meant to blend with all people of all races to teach understanding, compassion, and inclusion when seeing different faces.

That's what life is all about
by accepting others for who they are—
a very special part of the universe
as their own unique star.

This love letter ends with hope.
I pray my story has spoken to your heart
to teach you why albinos look different,
but are still part of God's enduring love,
filled with all races and colors sent
to earth from heaven above!

About the Authors

James O. Morehead is the senior pastor at Pasadena Heights Church of God in Indianapolis, Indiana. After 32 years, he retired as a tenured professor of the Communications Department from Anderson University in Anderson, Indiana. His teaching career began in 1969 in Oklahoma City, Oklahoma at John F. Kennedy Jr. and Northwest Classen high schools. In 1979, he was an Assistant Professor of Theater and Speech at his alma mater Grambling State University in Grambling, Louisana where he also directed plays, designed sets, sound, and lighting for campus productions. Morehead became the Chair of the Theater Department at Odessa College in Odessa, Texas in 1982.

He was the first African-American to receive a master's degree in Speech and Theater from Oklahoma State University in Stillwater, Oklahoma. While an undergraduate student at Grambling State, Morehead majored in Speech and Theater Education, performing in most of the campus plays, building scenery, and designing lights and sound. He was awarded "Best Actor" three times, and in 1968 won the "Outstanding Senior in Theater" award. He was introduced to the world of theater at age 14 at M. H. Carroll High School in Monroe, Louisana where he fell in love with William Shakespeare who wrote that "the play is the thing," and for Morehead there were no truer words. He says acting saved his life and brought him out of his introverted shell, and with costumes and makeup, he could become anyone the playwright created. He became somewhat of a high school celebrity because of his skilled acting.

Morehead married his college sweetheart Norma Jean Morehead, and they have two daughters - Andrea Morehead Allen and Amie Morehead. He has one grandchild, Ean James Allen.

Andrea Morehead Allen is a seven-time Emmy Award-winning television journalist for over 30 years having anchored weekday newscasts in Indianapolis, Grand Rapids, Michigan and Worcester, Massachusetts. She has field-anchored major events including the 2009 Inauguration of former U.S. President Barack Obama, 2002 Final Four in Atlanta, 2002 Winter Olympics in Salt Lake City, 2000 NBA Championships in Los Angeles, and the 2000 Summer Olympics in Sydney, Australia.

She is a cancer survivor and thriver after her diagnosis of triple negative breast cancer in 2018, and serves as a passionate advocate for early detection and education as a board member for Pink 4-Ever. The organization aims to reduce breast cancer late-stage diagnosis and death rates for black women in Indianapolis.

Allen is also a recipient of journalism's most prestigious award — an Edward R. Murrow, but her greatest life achievement is her son Ean James Allen.

About Marvin Jones III

Marvin Jones III, also known as Krondon, is an American actor and rapper from Los Angeles, California. He is a member of the group Strong Arm Steady, along with rappers Phil Da Agony and Mitchy Slick. As an actor, Jones is known for his amazing portrayal of the character Tobias Whale in The CW superhero television series Black Lightning, and as the voice of Tombstone in the superhero film Spider-Man: Into the Spider-Verse.

About the Illustrator

Stephanie Hider is a children's book illustrator currently living in Oklahoma with her daughter and maltipoo pup Neko. She is an avid gamer, Sci-fi geek and prolific reader whose favorite work is Plethora.